ANIMALS

COLORING BOOK FOR ADULTS

OANCEA CAMELIA

I0413909

This adult coloring book has 50 animal patterns, featuring creatures great and small from jungles, seas, sands and savannahs all around the world.

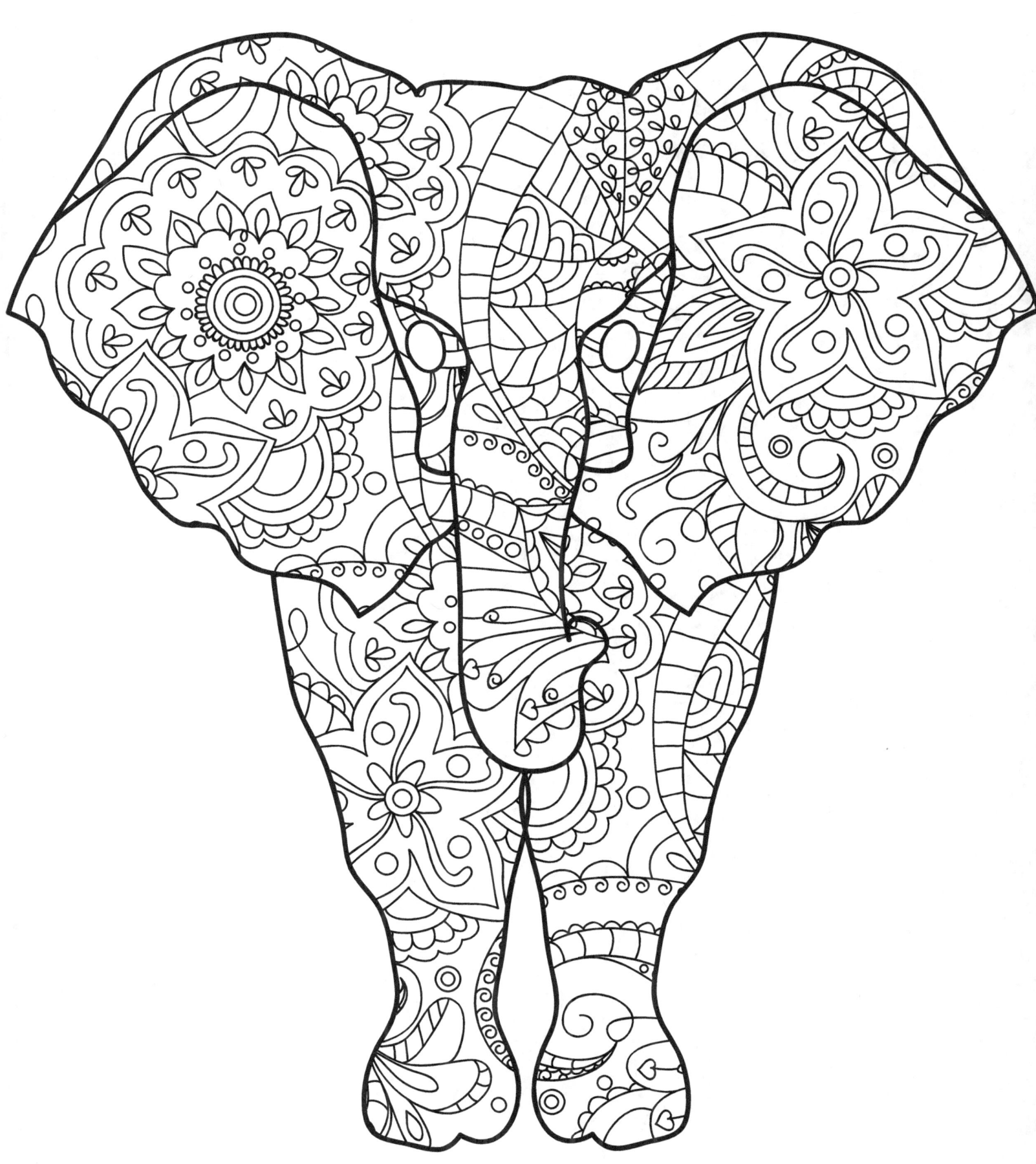

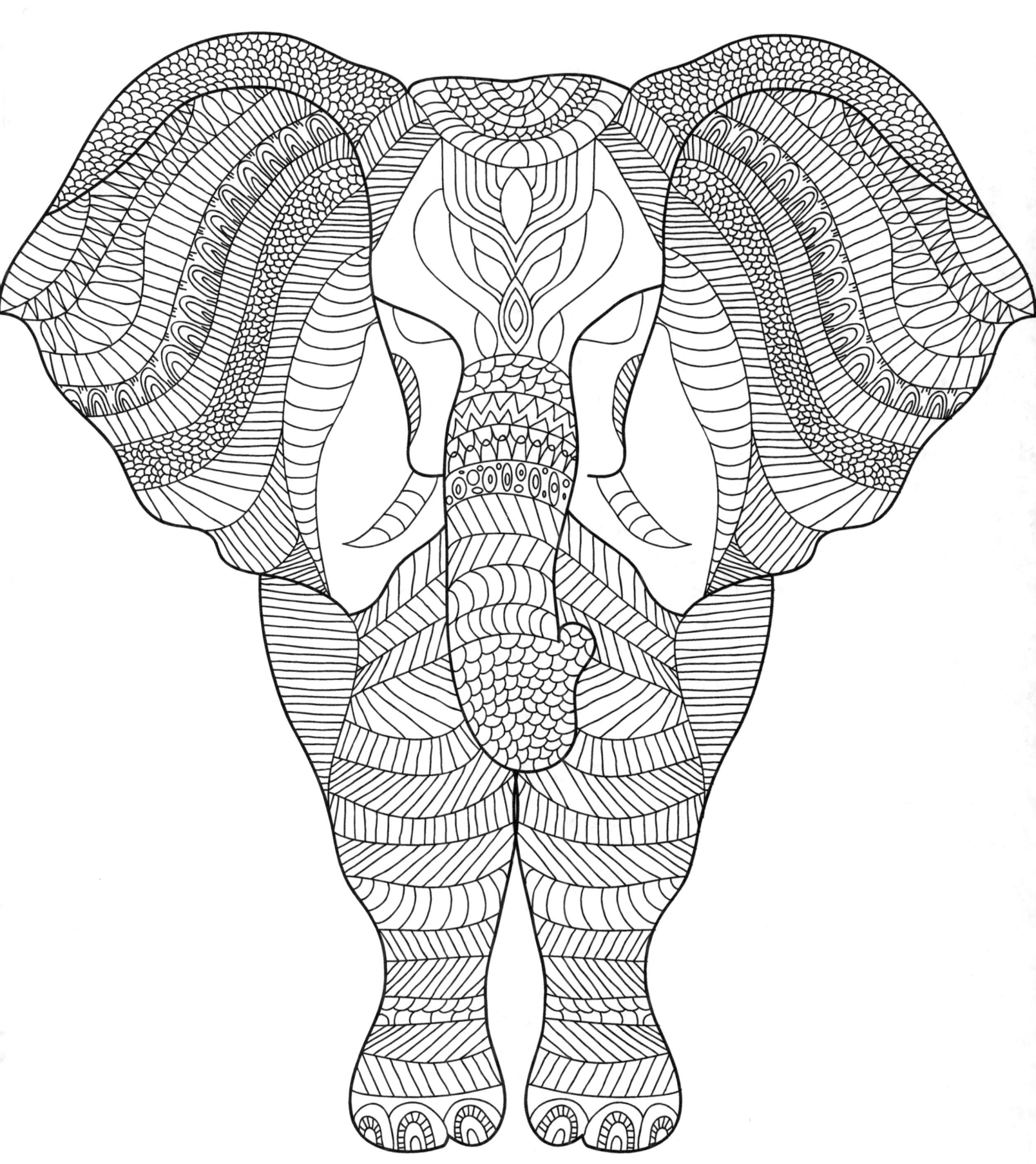

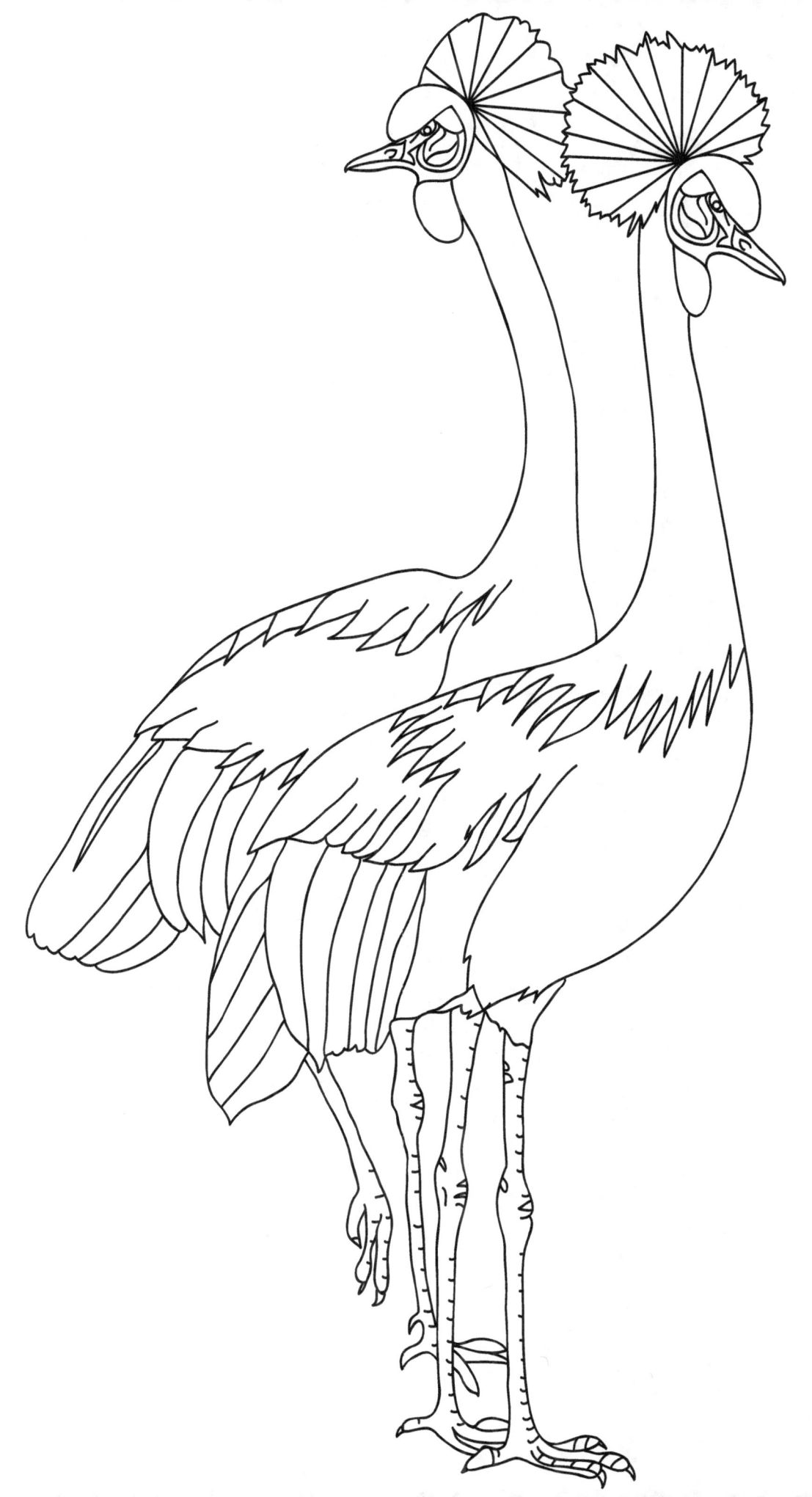

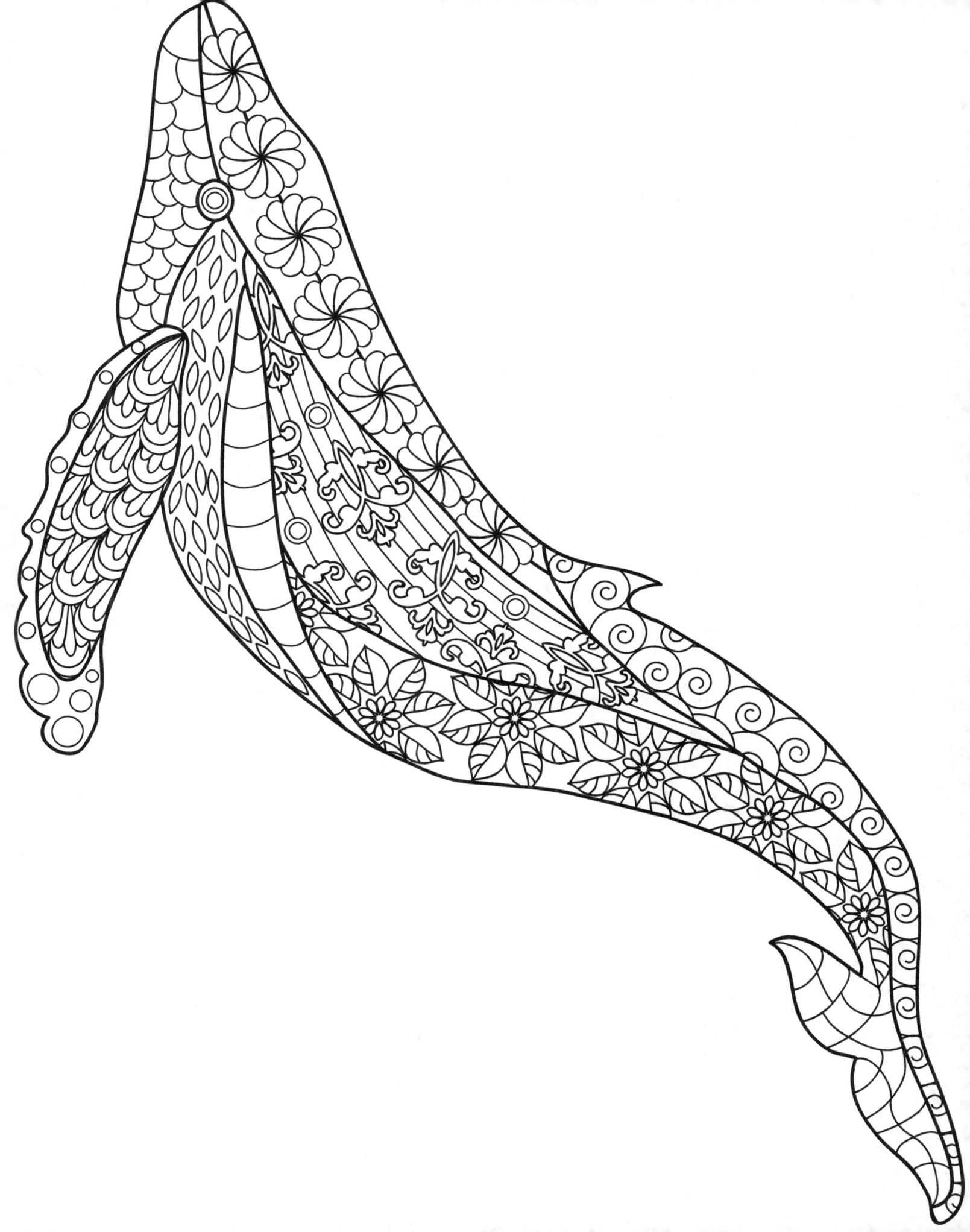

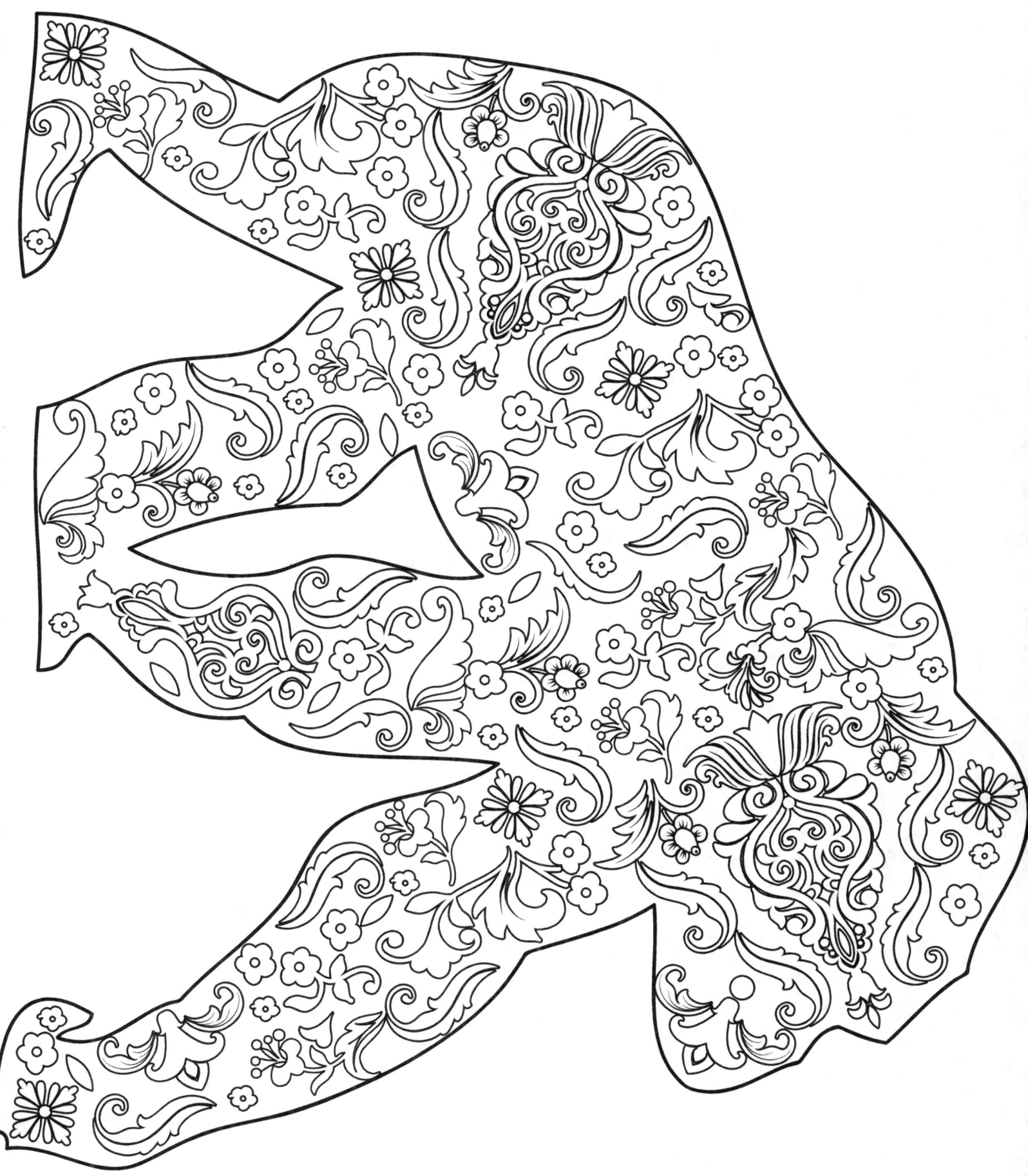

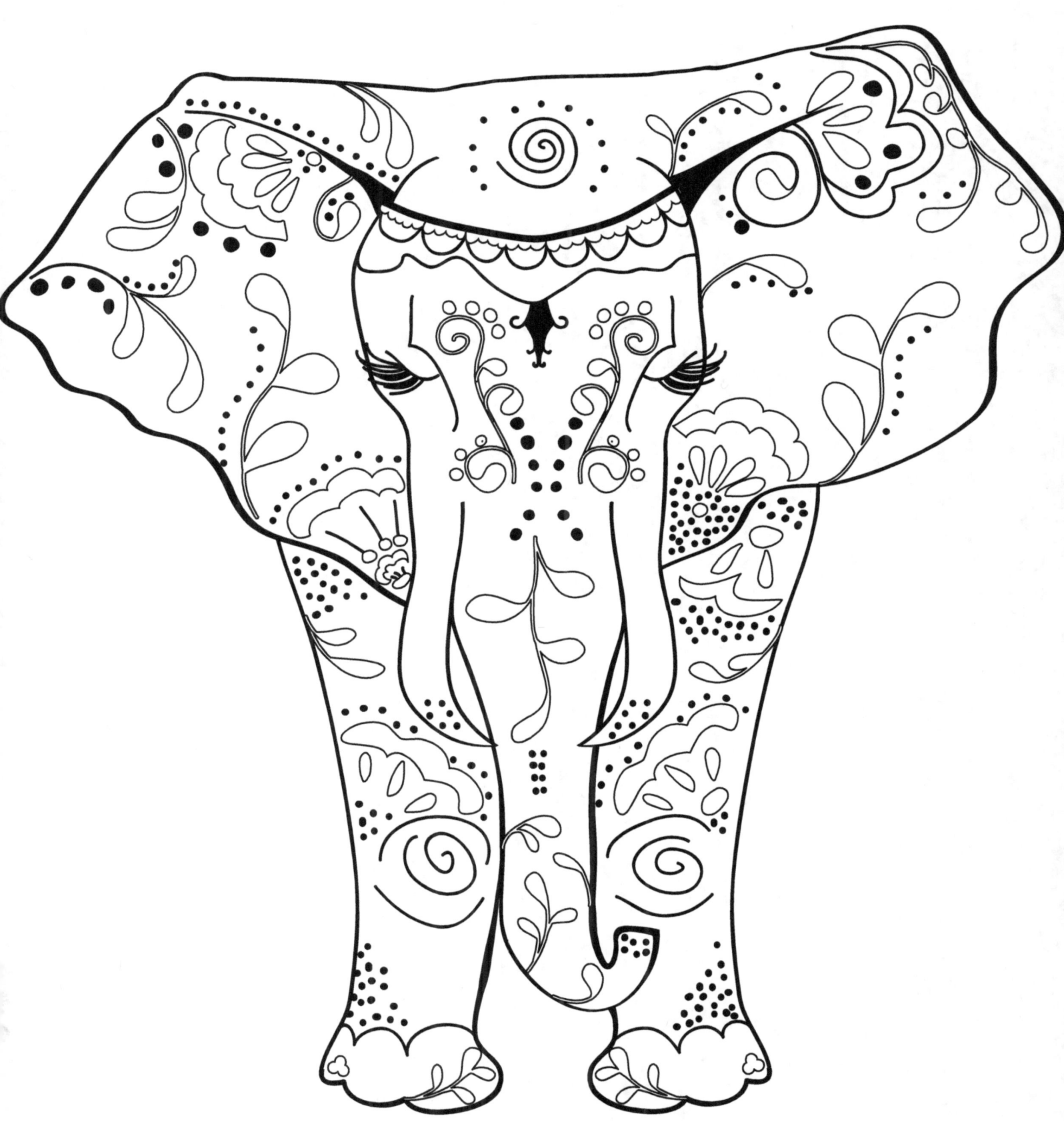

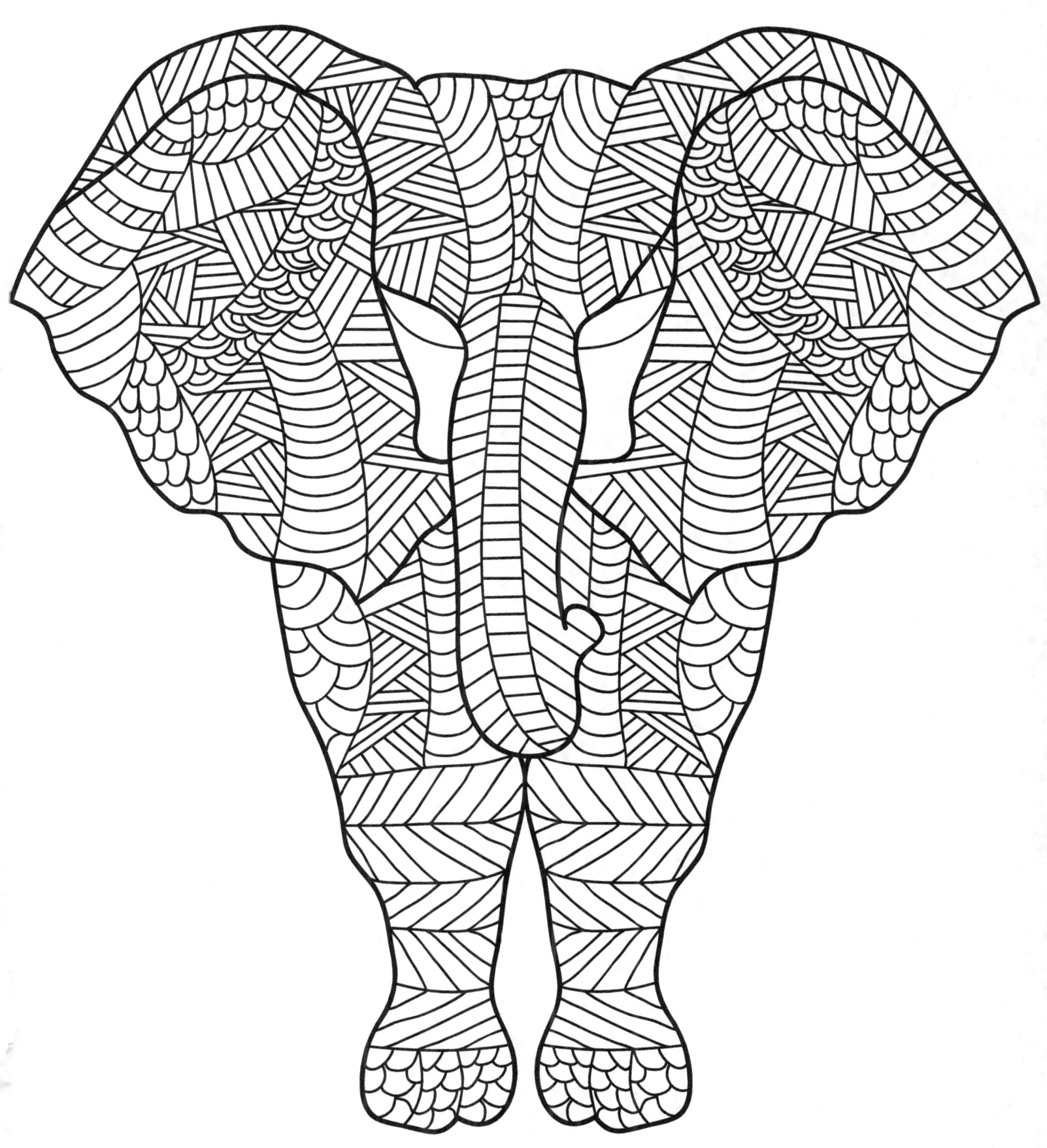